Simply Dance

Waltz and Quickstep

Rita Storey

W
FRANKLIN WATTS
LONDON·SYDNEY

Before you start

Dancing is a great way to get fit and meet people. Wherever you live there are likely to be dance classes held somewhere nearby. There are some steps in this book that you can try to get you started. There are also some suggestions for clips of music to listen to on pages 27–9.

You do not need a special costume to learn to dance. A pair of comfortable shoes and clothes that let you move easily will be fine to start with. It is not a good idea to wear trainers when you are dancing as the soles grip the floor and make it difficult to turn your feet easily. Some dance studios have their own dress code, so you might want to check what it is before turning up to a class.

When you are dancing it is a good idea to wear two or three thin layers of clothing. At the start of a dance session you need to keep your muscles warm to avoid damaging them when you stretch. As you get warmer you can take off some layers.

Like any type of physical exercise, dance has an element of risk. It is advisable to consult a healthcare professional before beginning any programme of exercise, particularly if you are overweight or suffer from any medical conditions. Before you begin, prepare your body with a few gentle stretches and exercises to warm you up.

Dancing is getting more and more popular. Give it a try and find out why!

First published in 2010 by
Franklin Watts
338 Euston Road
London NW1 3BH

Franklin Watts Australia
Level 17/207 Kent Street
Sydney NSW 2000

© Franklin Watts 2010
Series editor: Sarah Peutrill
Art director: Jonathan Hair

Series designed and created for Franklin Watts
by Storeybooks
Designer: Rita Storey
Editor: Nicola Barber
Photography: Tudor Photography

A CIP catalogue record for this book is available
from the British Library

Printed in China

Dewey classification: 793.3'3
ISBN 978 0 7496 9366 4

Picture credits
All photographs Tudor Photography, Banbury
unless otherwise stated.
Lebrecht Music and Arts Photo Library/Alamy
p4, Trinity Mirror/Mirrorpix/Alamy p26;
© Adrees Latif/Reuters/Corbis p17; ABC
Inc/Everett/Rex features pp5 and 16;
Shutterstock pp8, 15, 27, 28 1nd 29
Cover images Tudor Photography

All photos posed by models. Thanks to Jake
Thomas Chawner, and Lauren Cooper.

The Publisher would like to thank dance adviser
Kate Fisher (www.katefisherdanceacademy.com)
for her invaluable help and support.

Franklin Watts is a division of Hachette
Children's Books, an Hachette UK company
www.hachette.co.uk

Contents

Ballroom dances

Waltz and quickstep

Ballroom dances are performed by couples and recognised in competitions around the world. They are split into two groups: 'International Standard' and 'International Latin'. In International Standard ballroom dancing, the couples must spend most of the dance in a **closed hold** (facing each other, with both hands in contact with their partner). The waltz and quickstep are both International Standard ballroom dances.

Latin dances usually have a lot of hip action and rhythmic expression. They do not always have to be danced in a closed hold. The two partners in a couple may dance side-by-side, or even dance different moves from each other.

What is the waltz?

The waltz is the oldest of the ballroom dances. It has its origins in Austria in the 17th century. At first it was danced with the arms intertwined at shoulder height, later the closed hold was introduced. The word waltz comes from the old German word *walzen* meaning 'to turn', or 'to glide'.

The waltz came to Great Britain in 1816, when it was danced at the court of the **Prince Regent**. The young Queen Victoria was also very fond of the dance. By the middle of the 19th century, the waltz had become popular all over the world.

An improper dance?

Despite its growing popularity, there were many people who strongly disapproved of the the waltz. Other dances of the time were performed with little or no contact between the man and woman. The waltz was the first dance to introduce the **closed hold** – close contact between

The young Queen Victoria and her husband, Prince Albert, loved to dance the waltz. They helped to make it popular in Britain.

the two partners and with the man's arm around the woman's waist. This, and the fast, whirling movements of the waltz, were considered by many to make the dance unsuitable for young ladies.

Waltz music

In the 1830s two popular Austrian composers, Johann Strauss II and Franz Lanner, began to write waltz music. Johann Strauss composed so many pieces of music for the waltz that he became known as the 'Waltz King'.

Waltz styles

At the end of the 19th century a new style of waltz was introduced, called the Boston. It was slower than the original waltz, had fewer turns and longer steps. The Boston developed into the International style waltz that is performed in competitions today. The original fast-turning style of waltz became the **Viennese waltz**.

Monique Coleman learns to dance a waltz with her professional partner, Louis van Amstel, in *Dancing with the Stars*.

Waltz – the basics

The waltz is the most easily recognised of all the ballroom dances. It is a slow dance compared to some of the other dances, and its basic steps are easy to learn. Its style is gentle and romantic but if danced well it is also confident and stylish.

KEY

G The girl's steps

B The boy's steps

Boy and girl steps

'count' Count the moves as you dance them. You can count out loud at first if it helps.

A waltz practice exercise

Do this exercise on your own or alongside your partner before you try dancing the steps in hold.

one

two

three

1 Step back on to your right foot.

2 Step to the side on your left foot.

3 Close right foot to left foot.

Counting the steps

Waltz steps are counted **one**, two, three with the emphasis on 'one'. The basic steps of a waltz are step, step, close. The steps are long and the shoulders always stay parallel to the floor. Count **one**, two, three as you dance. Say '**one**' a little louder than 'two' and 'three'.

Waltz hold

In a waltz the couple dance facing their partner, with both hands in contact. This is called a ballroom or closed hold.

Waltz exercise

Before you begin to dance any waltz steps try the exercise shown on these two pages. You can dance this to music (see page 27) either on your own or with a partner.

This couple are in a closed hold ready to dance the waltz.

one

two

three

1 Step forwards on to your left foot.

2 Step to the side on your right foot.

3 Close left foot to right foot.

Waltz steps

The basic steps of a waltz are quite simple. As the dancers become more experienced there are many different variations to try. These include elegant turns, fast spins and sways.

Natural turn
Couples performing a waltz move around the floor anticlockwise as they dance. The two dancers in a couple also turn around each other. This step is

It is traditional for a bride and groom to have the first dance at their wedding. They usually try to dance a waltz.

Natural turn

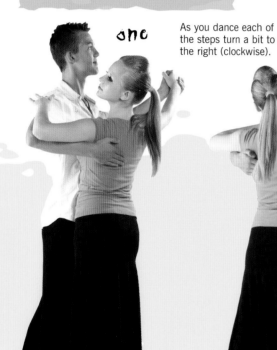

one

As you dance each of the steps turn a bit to the right (clockwise).

two

three

1 Step forwards on to your right foot.

1 Step back on to your left foot.

2 Step to the side with your left foot.

2 Step to the side with your right foot.

3 Close right foot to left foot.

3 Close left foot to right foot.

called a **natural turn** when the partners move around each other to the right (clockwise).

Rise and fall

As they perform a waltz, experienced dancers move up on to the balls of the feet and back down on to their heels – this is called rise and fall. The dancers 'rise' up on to the balls of the feet at the end of **beat** one, on to their toes on beat two, then 'fall' back so that their weight is on their heels on the third beat. Done properly this gives the dance a smooth up-and-down movement.

Waltz tip

Do not rush the steps in a waltz. The steps should be long and powerful but the dancers should make them look effortless and graceful as they glide around the dance floor.

one

two

three

4 Step back on to your left foot.

4 Step forwards on to your right foot.

5 Step to the side with your right foot.

5 Step to the side with your left foot.

6 Close left foot to right foot.

6 Close right foot to left foot.

Reverse turn

one

two

three

As you dance each of the steps turn a bit to the left (anticlockwise).

1 Step forwards on to your left foot.

1 Step back on to your right foot.

2 Step to the side with your right foot.

2 Step to the side with your left foot.

3 Close left foot to right foot.

3 Close right foot to left foot.

Reverse turn
A **reverse turn** is the opposite of a natural turn. The reverse turn in the waltz is a step in which the partners turn around each other to the left (anticlockwise).

one

two

three

4 Step back on to your right foot.

4 Step forwards on to your left foot.

5 Step to the side with your left foot.

5 Step to the side with your right foot.

6 Close right foot to left foot.

6 Close left foot to right foot.

Putting it together

The dance steps on pages 8–11 can be joined together to make a routine if you follow the sequence shown below.

Natural turn (pages 8–9)

As you dance each of the steps turn a bit to the right (clockwise).

one
1

two
2

three
3

one
4

two
5

three
6

Reverse turn (pages 10–11)

As you dance each of the steps turn a bit to the left (anticlockwise).

one

1

two

2

three

3

one

4

two

5

three

6

Then start the routine again from the beginning.

Waltz competitions and styles

The waltz and the Viennese waltz are both internationally recognised dances. This means that dancers from all over the world can compete against each other at a range of different levels.

Judging the waltz

When watching a waltz, judges are looking for elegance and smoothness. There should be rise and fall in the dance as well as lots of turns, spins and sways. The waltz is one of the most graceful ballroom dances, but this does not stop it being flamboyant and exciting to watch.

Costumes for dancing waltz

Dancers are judged on their appearance as well as their dancing ability. From the moment they walk on to the dance floor, dancers must display both confidence and style. Dancing the waltz is a wonderful excuse for girls to wear the most glamorous and elegant dresses. Flowing chiffon, glittering gems and sparkling jewellery are all part of the effect. Boys usually wear a classic **tail suit** with white bow tie. They must walk tall and have a smart and confident appearence.

This couple have put a lot of time, effort and expense into creating a good impression for the judges.

The Viennese waltz

The Viennese waltz that is danced in competitions today is almost twice as fast as the International Standard waltz. The dancers are constantly turning as they spin either clockwise or anticlockwise.

There are four basic steps in a traditional Viennese waltz. However, even though there are only a few steps, the Viennese waltz is not a suitable dance for beginners. To dance the Viennese waltz you must be very fit and have strong legs and ankles. The speed of the turns can also make you feel very dizzy until you get used to it!

American Smooth

In the USA the waltz and Viennese waltz are danced in the **American Smooth** version. In this version the dancers are allowed to dance in closed hold, open hold and even side-by-side. They have to keep in closed hold for only 40 per cent of the dance.

Viennese waltz fact

Couples dancing the Viennese waltz complete half a turn every three counts. A Viennese waltz is 60 counts per minute, so the dancers are turning 20 times a minute. To help prevent dizziness, the dancers spin first clockwise and then anticlockwise.

The movement of the fabric in a ballroom dance dress helps to show off the fast spins.

The American Smooth waltz recreates the glamour of movies made in Hollywood in the 1930s, particularly those starring Fred Astaire and Ginger Rogers. 'Fred and Ginger' made up possibly the most famous dancing partnership ever. Their dance style was a mix of ballroom, **tap** and **swing**.

Lifts

In some competitions and in showdances the American Smooth, routines can include lifts.

Steve Guttenberg and Anna Trebunskaya dance side-by side in *Dancing with the Stars*. This is allowed in an American Smooth waltz.

What is the quickstep?

The quickstep is one of the newest of the International Standard ballroom dances. It was developed in New York City, USA, and recognised as a ballroom dance in the 1920s. The quickstep is a very fast and energetic dance – not for the unfit!

Jazz and ragtime

In the 1920s **jazz** and **ragtime** were popular musical styles in the USA. In jazz clubs, people liked to dance the **foxtrot** to this music. The problem was that the foxtrot was originally a much slower dance and the dancers struggled to fit the steps to the faster speeds of jazz and ragtime music.

At about the same time a new dance sensation was sweeping Great Britain and the USA. It was called the **charleston**.

'Quick-time foxtrot and charleston'

To fit the steps of the foxtrot to the quicker tempo (speed) of the music, a fast foxtrot or 'quick-time foxtrot' was developed. This dance combined some elements from the charleston with the original foxtrot. At first it was known as the 'quick-time foxtrot and charleston'. With a bit of tidying up it became known as the 'quickstep'. The original foxtrot went back to its correct tempo and became the slow foxtrot.

China's Cao Jun and Liu Hong Mei fly across the dance floor as they dance the quickstep at the 4th East Asian Games.

Quickstep – the basics

Although it is danced quickly, the quickstep is an elegant ballroom dance. Its style is happy and lighthearted with quick, gliding footwork. It is one of the hardest dances to master, but a lot of fun to watch. It has jumps and hops, running steps and turns – all done at speed.

KEY

G The girl's steps

B The boy's steps

'count' Count the moves as you dance them. You can count out loud at first if it helps.

Quarter turn

Make a quarter turn to the right as you dance steps 1–4.

slow   *quick*   *quick*   *slow*

1 Step forwards on to your right foot.

1 Step back on to your left foot.

2 Step to the side with your left foot.

2 Step to the side with your right foot.

3 Close right foot to left foot.

3 Close left foot to right foot.

4 Step to the side on your left foot.

4 Step diagonally forwards on to your right foot.

Counting the steps

In the quickstep the steps are counted as slow and quick steps. The basic steps are easy to learn but there is also plenty for the more advanced dancer to master.

Quickstep hold

In a quickstep the couple dance facing their partner, with both hands in contact (ballroom or closed hold).

The dancer's **frame** (the position of the arms and upper body) remains still in a quickstep – the movement is all in the feet and legs.

quick

quick

Make a quarter turn to the left as you dance steps 5–8.

slow

slow

7 Close right foot to left foot.

7 Close left foot to right foot.

6 Step to the side with your left foot.

6 Step to the side with your right foot.

5 Step back on to your right foot.

8 Step forwards on to your left foot.

8 Step back on to your right foot.

5 Step forwards on to your left foot.

Quickstep steps

L earn these steps at a walking pace before you try to dance them to quickstep music. Start slowly and build up to the correct speed once you get more confident.

Promenade *chasse*

slow

quick

quick

slow

From step 2 get into **promenade position**. Turn the upper half of your body towards your left hand (boy), right hand (girl) .

4 Step to the side with your left foot.

4 Step to the side with your right foot.

1 Step back on to your right foot.

1 Step forwards on to your left foot.

2 Step to the side with your left foot.

2 Step to the side with your right foot.

3 Close right foot to left foot.

3 Close left foot to right foot.

Promenade step
In the promenade step the couple remain in hold but instead of dancing forwards or backwards facing each other, they dance the same step side-by-side, both facing in the same direction.

Chasse

Chasse steps are used in many different dances. *Chasse* means 'to chase'. In a *chasse* step one foot chases the other: step, close, step close. In a quickstep, the *chasse* step is danced in promenade position.

slow

quick

quick

slow

5 Step forwards and across with your right foot.

5 Step forwards and across with your left foot.

6 Step to the side with your left foot.

6 Step to the side with your right foot.

7 Close right foot to left foot.

7 Close left foot to right foot.

8 Step to the side with your left foot.

8 Step to the side with your right foot.

Quickstep tip

The skill of dancing a good quickstep is to make all the fast running steps, hops and turns look elegant and smooth as well as fun. A badly danced quickstep can look very 'skippy' and out of control.

Lock step

slow

quick

quick

1 Step forwards on to your right foot.

1 Step back on to your left foot.

2 Step forwards on to your left foot.

2 Step back on to your right foot.

3 Cross right foot behind left foot.

3 Cross left foot in front of right foot.

As you cross your feet go on to the balls of the feet and lock the back foot tightly behind the front foot.

The lock step
The **lock step** is a *chasse* step (step, close, step) in which one foot crosses closely behind the other and locks tight. Lock steps are used in the waltz, quickstep and **cha-cha**. They can be performed to the side (left and right), or to the front or back. Take care – it is easy to trip over, or trip your partner up, when dancing this step.

slow

Rise, fall and sway

Rise and fall is the up-and-down movement of a dance. In a quickstep, the rise and fall is created by dancing the slow steps on the heel, and the quick steps up on the toes. Sway is the curve of the body as the dancers move.

Frame

In ballroom dancing, the dancer's 'frame' is the position made by the upper body and arms. It is important for the dancers to have a good frame in order for the dance moves to be the correct shape. The frame in the waltz and quickstep should stay the same throughout the dance.

4 Step back on to your right foot.

4 Step forwards on to your left foot.

Quickstep tip

Your facial expression is important. The quickstep is a happy dance, so remember to smile!

Putting it together

The dance steps on pages 18–23 can be joined together to make a routine if you follow the sequence shown below.

Quarter turn (pages 18–19)

slow 1
quick 2
quick 3
slow 4
slow 5
quick 6
quick 7
slow 8

Promenade *chasse* (pages 20–21)

slow **1**

quick **2**

quick **3**

slow **4**

slow **5**

quick **6**

quick **7**

slow **8**

Lock step (pages 22–23)

slow **1**

quick **2**

quick **3**

slow **4**

Start the
routine again
from the
beginning.

25

Competition quickstep

In order for dancers to compete against each other in competitions, the steps of ballroom dances are set down in a syllabus that is taught in dance schools.

The quickstep in competition

The first priority for judges watching a competition quickstep is to look at the accuracy and speed of the steps. The dancers must have light, energetic steps that are completely in **unison** with each other as they move. The dance should be elegant as well as fast, giving the impression that the dancers' feet hardly touch the ground. The dance should not be skippy or jerky.

Musicality

Judges also look for musicality from dancing partnerships. The couple must be able to express the feeling of the music in the **choreography** of the dance and the way they perform. It is possible for a couple who dance very well to lose to another couple who interpret the music better.

Denise Lewis and Matthew Cutler dance a fast quickstep at the _Strictly Come Dancing_ roadshow.

Dance to the music

The music you dance to is very important. The regular beat, or pulse, of the music gives you the timing to move to. The rhythm and feel of the piece help you to perform the dance correctly.

Music for the waltz

The music for the waltz should be gentle and graceful. Many pieces of music use a full orchestra with strings and piano to give a rich melodic sound. Listen carefully and count the three beats in the music.

A full-size orchestra – sometimes called a symphony orchestra – can have as many as a hundred musicians.

Music for the Viennese waltz

The music of Johann Strauss II helped to make the waltz a popular dance in Vienna in the 19th century. His music is still popular with dancers today, although there are many other pieces of music suitable for dancing the Viennese waltz.

The most famous of Johann Strauss's pieces of waltz music is 'The Blue Danube'. This piece is played every year on New Year's Day, at the concert given by the Vienna Philharmonic Orchestra in Vienna, Austria.

Dance music Viennese waltz

A list of Viennese waltz music can be found on:
www.dancesportmusic.com/vw.html

Short clips for you to listen to:
www.ballroomdancers.com/Music/ search_style.asp?Dance=Viennese +Waltz

Other suggestions are:
'(Lough) Erin Shore', The Corrs
'Kiss from a Rose', Seal
'Ice Cream', Sarah McLachlan
'If I ain't Got You', Alicia Keys
'Time in a Bottle', Jim Croce
'Come Away with Me', Nora Jones

Dancers whirl around the floor at one of the magnificent New Year's balls held in Vienna, Austria.

Music for the quickstep

The music for a quickstep should be quick and light. The beat of the quickstep is the same as for a slow waltz (one, two, three), but while the waltz is played at 84 to 90 beats every minute the quickstep is played at 200 to 208 beats per minute.

The quickstep can be danced to many different styles of music. One type of music that fits the mood of the quickstep perfectly is swing music. This style of music became popular in the 1930s and 1940s. It is played by **big bands**. A big band typically has between 12 to 25 musicians with a brass section (trumpets, trombones) wind instruments (saxophones), a rhythm section (electric guitar, piano, double bass and drums) and singers.

Dance music
Quickstep

A list of quickstep music can be found on:
www.dancesportmusic.com/
quickstep.html

Short clips for you to listen to:
www.ballroomdancers.com/
Music/search_style.asp?
Dance=Quickstep

Other suggestions are:
'Suddenly I See', KT Tunstall
'Swing with Me', Jessica Simpson
'Down with Love', Michael Buble
& Holly Palmer

The music of a big band is a perfect accompaniment to the lively pace of a quickstep.

Glossary

American Smooth A version of the waltz, Viennese waltz, foxtrot or tango danced in competitions in the USA. The dancers are allowed to dance in closed hold, open hold and even side-by-side. These dances can also include lifts.

beat The regular pulse of a piece of music – like a heartbeat or a ticking clock.

big band A large group of musicians (typically between 12 and 25) playing trumpets, trombones, saxophones, electric guitar, piano, double bass and drums. Some big bands also have singers.

cha-cha An exciting Latin dance which originated in the 1950s in Cuba.

charleston An American dance popular in the 1920s. It incorporates fast kicking steps and swivelling foot movements.

chasse A step in which one foot chases the other: step, close, step, close.

choreography The arrangement and sequence of steps that form a dance.

closed hold (also called **ballroom hold**) A dance hold in which the two partners in a couple face each other and keep both hands in contact.

foxtrot A ballroom dance with a slow, slow, quick, quick rhythm.

frame The position of the arms and upper body while in dance position.

jazz A type of popular music that originated in New Orleans in America around 1900.

lock step A dance step in which one leg and foot is pulled in tightly to lock behind the other.

natural turn A dance step in which the partners turn to the right (clockwise).

Prince Regent A prince who takes the place of a reigning king or queen if he or she is unable to rule.

promenade position A dance position in which the dancer is ready to walk forwards.

ragtime An early form of jazz music.

reverse turn A dance step in which the partners turn to the left (anticlockwise).

swing A type of popular dance music based on jazz but played by big bands.

syllabus A summary of all the steps you need to learn for each dance medal or grade.

tail suit A type of suit worn by men at formal evening occasions. The jacket is long at the back and short at the front.

tap A dance in which each step is marked by a clicking noise, made by the metal part of the dancer's shoes (taps) on the floor.

unison Exactly together.

Viennese waltz A fast ballroom dance in which the couples turn constantly, often associated with the music of Johann Strauss II.

Further information

Websites

Steps to follow and lots of information about ballroom dances at www.ballroomdancers.com

Quickstep
www.ballroomdancers.com/dances/dance_overview.asp?Dance=QS

Waltz
www.ballroomdancers.com/Dances/dance_overview.asp?Dance=WAL

Viennese waltz
www.ballroomdancers.com/Dances/dance_overview.asp?Dance=VW

For action from the popular TV dance shows see:
www.bbc.co.uk/strictlycomedancing/
abc.go.com/shows/dancing-with-the-stars
www.fox.com/dance

Dance classes

Find a dance class wherever you are in the world:

www.dancesport.uk.com/studios_world/index.htm

DanceSport

Ten ballroom dances are referred to as the DanceSport dances. These dances are governed by internationally recognised rules and are danced in amateur and professional competitions around the world. There are five International Standard and five International Latin dances.

In the USA the American Smooth and American Rhythm correspond to the International Standard and International Latin classifications.

Note to parents and teachers

Every effort has been made by the Publishers to ensure that these websites are suitable for children, that they are of the highest educational value, and that they contain no inappropriate or offensive material. However, because of the nature of the Internet, it is impossible to guarantee that the contents of these sites will not be altered. We strongly advise that Internet access is supervised by a responsible adult.

Index